The Moon's Gorgonzola

Published by TROIKA
First published 2023
Troika Books Ltd, Well House, Green Lane, Ardleigh CO7 7PD, UK
www.troikabooks.com
Text copyright © Debra Bertulis 2023
Illustrations copyright © Zoe Williams 2023
The moral rights of the author and illustrator have been asserted
All rights reserved
A CIP catalogue record for this book is available
from the British Library
ISBN 978-1-912745-30-2

Printed in Poland at Totem.com.pl

The Moon's Gorgonzola

Poems by Debra Bertulis
Illustrations by Zoe Williams

troika

Contents

Space

Holiday In Space.................... 8
Just Star And Me 10

School

Show And Tell..................... 11
Miss's Magic Carpet 12
Ten Tired Teachers................ 14
Late For School................... 15
Headteacher Breaks The Rules 16
Sports Day Superhero.............. 18
Carpet Keep Fit................... 20

Feelings/Relationships

Best Friends...................... 21
Sometimes, When I Miss You........ 22
New School....................... 23

Nature/Mini Beasts

Fireflies......................... 24
Minibeasts....................... 25
My Garden........................ 26
Where My Field Used To Be 27
Poor Scarecrow 28

Weather

Whatever The Weather 30
It's A Welly Walk Day. 32
The Night Jeweller 33

Seaside

Sitting At The Harbour. 34
Train Ride To The Sea. 36
Shell In My Hand. 39

Food

Chocolate Spread 40
Ghost For Tea 41
What Food Am I? 42

Family

Grandma's Glasses 43
Mum's Jungle Trip 44
Two Of Everything. 45
Nanny Rose And Me 46
Land Of Bongoboz. 48
Dad's SO Embarras-SING. 50

Animals

My Kitten. 52
Who Am I? 53

Little Dreams 54
I'm a… 56
Swallow Song 59
Croc And Mole 59
What Is That Hullabaloo?. 60
Diary Of A Dog. 62
Diary Of A Cat 63
Diary Of A Mouse 64
Diary Of A Goldfish 65
Dinosaurs Are NOT Extinct 66

Festivals

Firework Night 68
Chinese Festival Dragon. 70
Celebrating YOU 72

More to Munch On

Just Write 73
Fafflefuffs 74
Pyjama Drama 76
When I Am Crowned King. 78
Journey Of A Smile 80
Broccoli Price 82
Eye Test. 84
Help Me Write A Poem. 86
Listen 87
Great Fire Of London September 2nd 1666 . . 88

*To Martin, Louisa and Natasha
With love*

Holiday In Space

I was so excited
When I booked a mini break
A galactic experience
A holiday in space!

Arrived safe and sound
Wasn't too impressed
The Moon's Gorgonzola
Cheddar's the best!

Tried to park on a star
What a joke
My rocket was melting
You should have seen the smoke!

Mars was sold out
Of my favourite choc
Aliens on half term
They'd scoffed the lot!

Jupiter greeted me
With a fairground ride
Spun me around
Sent me goggle eyed!

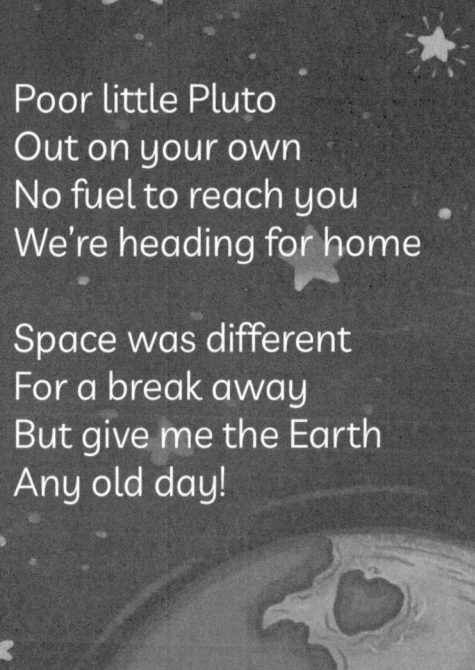

Poor little Pluto
Out on your own
No fuel to reach you
We're heading for home

Space was different
For a break away
But give me the Earth
Any old day!

Just Star And Me

Why can't I touch you, little star?
You don't look that far away
I can see you winking at me
You're asking me up to play

One day I will fly to meet you
Until the time I do
We'll play our winking game together
Just me, little star — and you.

Show And Tell

Today at school it's Show and Tell
But Ted is hiding from me
He's not in my wardrobe
He's not in my drawers
Where could he possibly be?

Today at school it's Show and Tell
But Ted is hiding from me
He's not under the bed
He's not *in* my bed
Where could he possibly be?

All of a sudden, there he is
Sitting by the front door
Ted was so excited for Show and Tell
That he wasn't lost at all!

Miss's Magic Carpet

This morning something happened
As we sat on the carpet in class
The carpet wriggled and jiggled
Then flew upwards really fast

Whoosh!

It zoomed us out of the window
Through the car park and down the lane
Over the English Channel to France
To the white sandy beaches of Spain

Whoosh!

We built an igloo in Antarctica
Climbed the mountains of Nepal
Saw the pyramids in Egypt
Made friends in Senegal

Whoosh!

We rode a camel through the Sahara
Watched fireflies dance in Nice
Bought gifts at a souk in Morocco
Bathed in the sea in Greece

Whoosh!

We trekked through the Amazon Rainforest
The Great Wall of China, too
Gazed at the tulips in Amsterdam
Visited Timbuktu

Whoosh!

We met a leprechaun in Ireland
Watched beautiful fountains in Rome
Had a gondola ride in Venice
Then

Whoosh!

Back to the
Classroom we go.

WHOOSH!

Ten Tired Teachers

Ten tired teachers
Yawning during break
Suddenly spring to life
When they hear the word
CAKE!

Ten tired teachers
In the staff room sleep
Suddenly spring to life
When they hear the word
SWEETS!

Ten tired teachers
In a sleepy dream
Suddenly spring to life
When they hear the words
ICE CREAM!

Ten tired teachers
Enjoying a lovely doze
Just doze doze doze
When the bell goes!

Late For School

Today felt very strange indeed
Our morning alarm didn't ring
We all slept in and got up late
What an awful state we were in

We all dressed in a panic
My brother couldn't find his tie
My school skirt was out on the washing line
It wasn't even dry

Back at home at four o' clock
Before we change for tea
Mum points at us in horror
Not believing what she sees

'You've been to school in your slippers
The shark ones with furry teeth!
You've worn your summer shorts to school
With your trousers underneath!'

There had to be an answer
Then my sister yelled 'I know!
We'll all be on time tomorrow
Because tonight we'll sleep in our clothes!'

Headteacher Breaks The Rules

Our Headteacher, Mr Wright
Says every single day
'Walk don't run, it's not allowed!'
But what did HE do today?

He RAN like the wind from the art room
CHARGED like a bull through PE
TORE like an athlete into lunch
Yelling
Hungry! Hungry! Hungry!

He JOGGED down the corridor with his nose in the air
HOPPED like a frog to Class Two
CARTWHEELED through Nursery, scaring the tots
Yelling
Zoom! Zoom! Zoom!

He WHIRLED round the hall like a ballet dancer
SPRINTED into Class One
JUMPED into the kitchen, frightening the cook
Yelling
Fun! Fun! Fun!

All the secretaries tell him off
For breaking the 'No Running' rule
But oh no! There he goes again
Vroom, Vroom, Vroom!

For More Fun...
Make this poem even more fun by adding the name of your own Headteacher!

Sports Day Superhero

I can't fly through the air
Or twist upside down
I can't do a cartwheel
Or hang upside down

I can't run a mile
Or around a track
I can't jump a hurdle
Or do things like that

I can't throw the discus
Or play basketball
I can't swim a length
Or swim AT ALL!

But...

I can be a supporter
In more ways than one
I can cheer on my friends
Tell them 'well done!'

Award yourself Gold
If this sounds like you
You're a Sports Day Superhero
Through and through!

Carpet Keep Fit

Skip on the carpet
Hop on the carpet
Jump on the carpet
FLOP!

Bend on the carpet
Twist on the carpet
Stretch on the carpet
DROP!

Wriggle on the carpet
Squiggle on the carpet
Giggle on the carpet
PLOP!

Creep on the carpet
Stomp on the carpet
Stand still on the carpet
STOP!

Best Friends

Saniyah and I are best friends
Ben says Saniyah's his best friend too
But Saniyah is my best friend not Ben's
What am I going to do?

When Saniyah asks me to play
Sometimes she asks Ben too
Sometimes Ben tells me to 'go away'
What am I going to do?

Ben sits by Saniyah at lunch time
He stands next to her in the queue
I have no one to sit by
What am I going to do?

Sometimes, When I Miss You

I'm a...

Car without an engine
A boat without an oar
A ship without a sail
A house without a door

I'm a...

A fish without a fin
A wave without a sea
A crab without a shell
A lock without a key

I'm a...

A bee without a buzz
A horse without its hay
A petal with no flower
A night without its day.

Sad Poems
Write down how you feel when you're missing someone and what you miss about them.

New School

I've started a new school today
I didn't want to leave my bed
My tummy was churning upside down
I wanted to stay home instead

I was worried about making friends
That they wouldn't like me
Worried what happens at snack time
Worried about how I'd feel

When mummy left me at the door
My tummy did a flip
Then I asked someone to be my friend
And the day flew by so quick!

So remember when anything is new
It may feel like a scary day
But ask someone to be your friend
Then your worries will go away.

Fireflies

Fireflies twinkle
Under moonlit skies
Blinking
Winking
Through the air they fly

Fireflies dance
Under starry skies
Twirling
Whirling
On the breeze they ride

Fireflies sparkle
Under diamond skies
Glinting
Glistening
Through the trees they glide.

> Fireflies are a kind of beetle, although they look like little darting flies, which shine like tiny torches at night. I first saw them on holiday in the South of France on a very warm summer's evening. They gave a spectacular light show and danced around us!

Minibeasts

Tiny ants
Under a leaf
Looking for insects
And flies to eat

Tiny beetles
Under a stone
Keep warm and safe
In their cosy home

Tiny woodlice
Inside a log
Feed on seeds
In the damp of a bog

Tiny snail
In the vegetable patch
Leaves a trail
To find his way back

All kinds of places
Minibeasts thrive
Open your eyes
See what you find!

My Garden

A garden is an orchestra
When the moon wakes
Of sounds not heard in the day

The snort of a badger
The hoot of an owl
A harmony lulls us to sleep
Shh Shh
A harmony lulls us to sleep

My garden is a symphony
When the sun wakes
Of sounds not heard at night

The chirruping chaffinch
The blackbird's tune
All to sing us awake
Tweet tweet
All to sing us awake.

Where My Field Used To Be

I ploughed this field for many years
Grew golden corn and wheat
Rabbits, moles and field mice
Thrived with lots to eat

Badgers built their cosy sets
Beneath the shady trees
Wild flowers gifted pollen
To butterflies and bees

Their habitat destroyed now
As far as my eye can see
Only homes for humans sit
Where my field used to be.

Poor Scarecrow

I'm pleased I'm not a scarecrow
Standing in a field all day
Where birds are nesting
With no voice to shoo them away

I'm glad I'm not a scarecrow
Standing in a field all day
Where birds are nesting
Mice are sleeping
With no voice to shoo them away

I'm thankful I'm not a scarecrow
Standing in a field all day
Where birds are nesting
Mice are sleeping
Spiders are weaving
With no voice to shoo them away

Don't you feel sorry for scarecrows
Standing in a field all day
Where birds are nesting
Mice are sleeping
Spiders are weaving
Worms are slithering

Whatever The Weather

Hold on to your woolly hat
Howled the wind
I am the wildest storm
I will blow the hair off your head
Run home, you have been warned

Wooo Woooo!
Wooo Woooo!

Find your winter scarf
Blew the snow
Wear your warmest clothes
I will freeze the tips of your fingers
I will freeze the tips of your toes

Shiver shiver!
Shiver shiver!

Find your waterproof coat
Poured the rain
Bring out your largest umbrella
I will bring floods and puddles
I will bring the soggiest weather

Splish splash!
Splish Splash!

WAIT!

Find your swimming costume
Find your buckets and spades
The sun is finally out
We'll play at the beach all day.

It's A Welly Walk Day

Who's for a welly walk
A splishy splashy welly walk
A jumping in the puddles walk
A welly walk today?

Splishy
Splashy
Splishy
Splashy

Who's for a welly walk
A squishy squashy welly walk
A jumping in the mud walk
A welly walk today?

Squishy
Squashy
Squishy
Squashy

Splish
Splash
SPLOSH!

IT'S A WELLY WALK DAY!
YAY!

The Night Jeweller

When the moon is clear in a cloudless sky
When the air is cold as ice
The Night **J**eweller sets to work
All through the freezing night

We wake to a **C**arpet of diamonds
Crystals that spar**K**le like stars
He ices the roo**F**tops of houses
Coats the windscreens of cars

Bejewels the top of the church spi**R**e
Showers the road to school
Ad**O**rns the hedgerows with tinsel
With glinting, twinkling jewels

As the moon is clear in a cloudles**S** sky
Who makes this treasure chest?
Who is **T**he Night Jeweller?
Can anybody guess?

Answer: Jack Frost

Sitting At The Harbour

Sitting at the harbour
What can we see?
Little boats bobbing
On a glistening sea

Bob Bob
Bob Bob

Sitting at the harbour
What can we hear?
Squawking seagulls
Picking scraps off the pier

Squawk squawk
Squawk squawk

Sitting at the harbour
What do we taste?
Salty chips salty lips
Salty hands and face

Yum Yum
Yum Yum

Sitting at the harbour
What do we smell?
Fish from my fishing net
Crabs and cockleshells

Sniff Sniff
Sniff Sniff

Sitting at the harbour
What do we say?
Please can we stay
For another day?

Senses Poems
I see, I hear, I smell, I taste... is a great starter for a poem. Close your eyes and let your imagination take you there.

Train Ride To The Sea

We're off to the sea
On the train today
Bucket and spades
Buckets and spades!

We're off to the sea
On the train today
To catch some crabs
To catch some crabs!

We're off to the sea
On the train today
Fish and chips
Fish and chips!

We see the sea
On the train today
Nearly there
Nearly there!

We're slowing down
On the train today
Time to get off
Time to get off!

We're at the beach
We're at the beach
Ice creams to eat
Ice creams to eat!

Time to go home
On the train today
Memories to keep
Memories to keep.

Performance Tips

When we repeat lines, it makes those lines stand out. Where will your train ride take you? What will you see? Trains speed up and slow down, so show this in your actions and voices.

Shell In My Hand

The shell in my hand
Takes me back to the sea
Back to sand in my toes
Fish and chips for tea

Back to the warmth
Of summer days
Salty sea air
Ocean spray

The shell in my hand
Takes me back to the sea
I just have to hold it
And there I will be.

Chocolate Spread

Oh!

Chocolate spread
Chocolate spread
I love you to pieces
Chocolate spread

I eat you in the bath
I eat you in bed
Pass me the jar
Of my chocolate spread

I love you
I love you
Straight from the spoon
On a hot sandy beach
In a windswept monsoon

Skiing down a mountain
Paddling in the sea
ANYTIME, ANYWHERE
Chocolate spread for ME!

Ghost For Tea

A ghost came to ours for tea last night
Sat clear as day in the chair
Helped himself to the last of the cake
Which I thought was a bit unfair.
'Who invited you?' I asked
'I need no invitation
Ghosts like me can just appear
As we feel the inclination.'
He said he'll come tomorrow
If we have angel cake
I said on one condition
That he teaches himself how to bake!

What Food Am I?

Study the clues
If you are a **b** le
To find
Something
You may eat
At a dining table...

I am long
I am sho **r** t
I am cold
I am hot
I am brown
I am white
V **e** getable
I am not
I am round
I am squ **a** re
I am soft
I am hard
Sometimes
A sol **d** ier
Standing guard...

Answer: Bread

> **Performance Tip**
>
> Performing for school? Put the adults in the audience to the test with this puzzle poem!

Grandma's Glasses

When we stay with Grandma
We play her favourite game
'Can you find my glasses
I've lost them again!'

Whilst Grandma has her snooze
And sits quietly in her chair
We're looking in her pot plants
We're looking everywhere

We peer into her handbag
And down the sofa too
We look inside the rabbit hutch
And even down the loo!

We didn't find them in her greenhouse
We didn't find them in her bed
Because whilst Grandma's quietly snoozing
They are sitting on her head!

Mum's Jungle Trip

Mum said she'd been on a trip
To the jungle for the day
I didn't know the jungle was close enough
I thought jungles were far away

Mum said the jungle is very near
But said she'd never go back
The experience left her petrified
The jungle was smelly and black

The jungle floor was covered with
Stuff she couldn't un-see
Stale food, smelly socks
What a dreadful place to be

When I came home from school
I found a note on my bedroom door
**YOUR BEDROOM IS A JUNGLE
TIDY YOUR BEDROOM FLOOR!**

Two Of Everything

I have two mums
I have two dads
It's a very special thing
Two bedrooms
Two houses
Two of everything
I am only one
They all share me
Twice the love,
Twice the joy
Lucky, lucky me.

Nanny Rose And Me

*(For Rosemary Griffith and her granddaughter
Rosie Abigail Griffith)*

Welcome to my garden
There is so much to see
Hold my hand, I'll show you
Just Nanny Rose and me.

Smell the perfume, Nanny
Of this rose my daddy grew
Petals soft as feathers
As soft and sweet as you!

Lift the flower, gently
Hold it to your nose
A flower for my Nanny
Shall we call it 'Nanny's Rose'?

I've picked us both some daisies
To make a daisy crown
We're going to look so beautiful
Come on, Nanny, sit down.

Look at our lovely daisy crowns
Haven't we been clever!
I'll wear yours and you wear mine
Daisy Queens together!

Say you'll come tomorrow
For a picnic under the tree
We'll chat about all kinds of things
Just Nanny Rose and me.

Land Of Bongoboz

Today in the land of Bongoboz
You can hear the Bongoboz snore
Which shakes his Bongoboz windows
And rattles his Bongoboz door

Today in the land of Bongoboz
The Bongoboz is awake
You can smell the Bongoboz cooking chips
And the Bongoboz frying steak

Today in the land of BongoBoz
You can hear his Xbox boom
The Bongoboz spends all day
In his Bongoboz bedroom

The Bongoboz is very weird
The Bongoboz is like no other
Who is this noisy Bongoboz?
The Bongoboz is my brother!

Dad's SO Embarras-SING

Help!

My dad is mistaken
He thinks he can sing
He sings all the time
He's SO EMBARRAS-SING!

HELP!

Dad sings on the loo
In the bath
In his shed
To his wallet
His toenail
To the hat on his head

To the dog down the lane
To the neighbour's gate
To the clock in our lounge
To his dinner plate

HELP!

While eating spaghetti
While drinking tea
Dad sings to the pot plants
To the laundry

To his toothbrush
To his toothpaste
To his Mickey Mouse pants
To the freckle on his nose
To a passing ant

HELP!

My dad is mistaken
He thinks he can sing
Dad! STOP SINGING!
You're SO EMBARRAS-SING!!

My Kitten

My kitten is so naughty
She scratches at the door
Unravels Mummy's knitting
Makes puddles on the floor

The only time she's good
Is when she's fast asleep
So quietly by her basket
We creep, creep, creep!

Who Am I?

I'm a weird loOking thing
And a little bit shy
I sit inside coral
To watCh sea-life go by

I hold out my arms
But I don'T want a hug
I have three hearts
And blue bloOd

I have nine brains
I am suPer bright
I can live till I'm five
I change coloUr at night

I am not a fish
Though I live in the sea
The number 'eight'
Is Special to me.

Answer: Octopus

Little Dreams

Little hamster
Little hamster
Spinning on his wheel
Dreams of tasty dandelions
On his hamster wheel

Spin Spin
Spin Spin

Little mouse
Little mouse
In his attic home
Dreams of chocolate and cheese
In his attic home

Dream Dream
Dream Dream

Little bunny
Little bunny
Hopping in his hutch
Dreams of tasty carrots
Hopping in his hutch

Hop Hop
Hop Hop

Little hamsters
Little mice
Little hopping bunnies
Dream all day of tasty food
To fill their hungry tummies!

I'm a...

I'm a cute cuddly puppy
That everybody loves
Woof woof woof

I'm a fluffy furry kitten
That everybody loves
Purr purr purr

I'm a hoppy happy rabbit
That everybody loves
Twitch twitch twitch

I'm a graceful gliding duck
That everybody loves
Quack quack quack

I'm a pink and porky pig
That everybody loves
Grunt grunt grunt

I'm a HUGE hairy tarantula
That not everybody loves
Creep creep creep
RUN!

Swallow Song

Today I freed my swallow
With her mended broken wing
Back into a cloudless sky
I'm sure I heard her sing.

Croc And Mole

Croc said to mole in a sly voice
'Hop on to my back!'

'No thanks' said mole, crossly
'Find a different snack!'

What Is That Hullabaloo?

Ethel the Elephant
Was in a bad mood
She stomped through the jungle
Calling

WHAT IS THAT HULLABALOO?

Hey you up there, Cockatoo!
She bellowed
Are you the hullabaloo?

No, said Cockatoo
I'm perched up here in my tree
Quietly eating berries
That noise is not coming from me

WHAT IS THAT HULLABALOO?

Hey you up there, Chimp!
She yelled
Are you the hullabaloo?

No, said Chimp
I'm just swinging around
Munching my tasty fruit
It's not me making that sound

WHAT IS THAT HULLABALOO?

Hey you down there, Hyena!
She shrieked
Are you the hullabaloo?

No, laughed Hyena
I can't help my grin
I'm chilling in my den
It's not me making that din

Well, who is it then?
Screeched Ethel
If it isn't any of you?

Ethel, they all said together
There is indeed a hullabaloo
If you listen very carefully

The hullabaloo is **YOU!**

Diary Of A Dog

Monday: Chased a cat in a field through a hedge.

Tuesday: Chased a cat into next-door's garden.

Wednesday: Ran out of the front door to chase a cat down the lane.

Thursday: Disturbed a cat sunning itself then chased the cat onto the top of a car.

Friday: Saw a cat quietly washing itself. Chased it.

Saturday: Chased two cats minding their own business on a roof.

Sunday: Lie in. A bone for breakfast. (Dreamed of chasing cats.)

Diary Of A Cat

Monday: Chased a mouse stealing cheese.

Tuesday: Chased a mouse.

Wednesday: Chased a mouse hiding in the grass.w

Thursday: Chased a mouse sitting on a log.

Friday: Sheltered from the rain. When it stopped, I... chased a mouse.

Saturday: Sunned myself. Chased a mouse.

Sunday: Day off. Cream for breakfast. Snoozed. (Dreamed of chasing mice.)

Diary Poems
List the days of the week. Who/What are you going to write about? An animal or your friend, your mum/dad?

Diary Of A Mouse

Monday: Chased by a cat.

Tuesday: Chased by a cat down the road.

Wednesday: Chased by two cats down the road.

Thursday: Chased by the same cat from Monday down the road and into a field.

Friday: Chased by next door's kittens!! Who DO they think they are!

Saturday: Minding my own business, was chased by a cat through a crack in the skirting board.

Sunday: Had a terrible dream that Monday's cat caught me! Oh no!

Diary Of A Goldfish

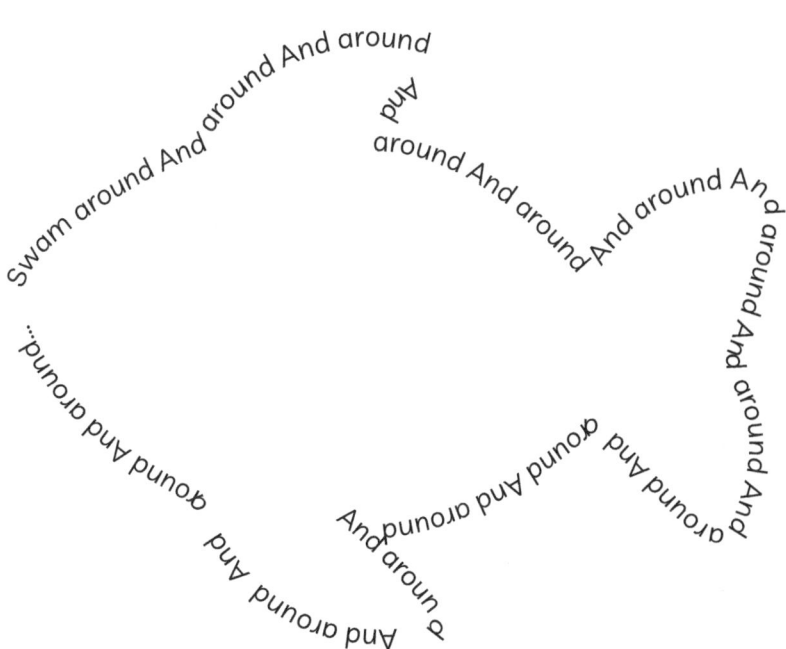

Dinosaurs Are NOT Extinct

There's a dinosaur sleeping
In the room next to me
It snores all night
Like a foghorn at sea

Whistle
Whistle
Snore
Snore

I've never actually seen it
The dinosaur next door
But I know he's definitely in there
Because I hear him snore

Whistle
Whistle
Snore
Snore

I've tried to tell Mum
I've tried to tell Dad
They just laugh out loud
They think I'm mad

Whistle
Whistle
Snore
Snore

Dinosaurs do exist
I have the proof
Because it snores its head off
Under my roof!

Whistle
Whistle
Snore
Snore.

Firework Night

Do you want to be a firework
In the night sky?
Do you want to be a firework?
Come on, let's fly!

We are...

a sparkler that sizzles

a fountain of fizz

a rocket that races

a firecracker whizz

a Catherine Wheel spinning

an exploding flower

a trail of colour

a glittering shower

See our colours
See us fly
An explosion of wonder
In a rainbow sky.

Chinese Festival Dragon

The Festival Dragon dances
The Festival Dragon prances
The Festival Dragon has many feet
To dance and prance
Through the festival streets

The Festival Dragon leaps
The Festival Dragon creeps
The Festival Dragon has many feet
To leap and creep
Through the festival streets

The Festival Dragon twirls
The Festival Dragon whirls
The Festival Dragon has many feet
To twirl and whirl
Through the festival streets.

Celebrating YOU

We celebrate on Mother's Day
We celebrate Father's Day too
So many people to celebrate
So how about celebrating YOU?

Hurrah for your loving, caring side
Hurrah for your loyalty
Hurrah for your sense of humour
Hurrah for your honesty

Hurrah for helping your friend to smile
Hurrah for being kind
Hurrah for making a difference
Hurrah for your sunshine

Take a moment to celebrate
Things that you say and do
For you are the only YOU on Earth
So how about celebrating YOU?

Just Write

Funny poems
Sad poems
Poems about your dad poems
Silly poems
Zany poems
Poems about your mum poems
Long poems
Short poems
Squiggly wriggly worm poems
Any kind of poem
Any kind of poem
ANY kind of poem
Is the one that's
JUST WRITE!

Fafflefuffs

Here we are in the land of Fafflefuff
Where Fafflefuffs are at play
They speak the language of Fafflefuff
In their own Fafflefuff Fafflefuff way

Fafflefuff! Fafflefuff! Fafflefuff!

If a Fafflefuff wants its breakfast
It says 'Fafflefuff! Fafflefuff!' twice
Then the Fafflefuff gobbles up his cereal
Fafflefuff puffed rice

When a Fafflefuff feels happy
It squeals 'Fafflefuff! Fafflefuff *weee!*'
Then the Fafflefuff spins around the room
As happy as a Fafflefuff can be!

Now say 'Fafflefuff fafflefuff fafflefuff?'
There! You said *'how do you do?'*
'Fafflefuff fafflefuff fafflefuff'
Now you speak Fafflefuff, too!

FAFFLEFUFF!

Draw your Fafflefuff and give it a name, imagining what it likes to eat or what games it plays, where it sleeps, what naughty things it gets up to.

Pyjama Drama

Pink pyjamas
Green pyjamas
Blue pyjamas
Red
Which colour pyjamas
Shall I wear to bed?

Shall I choose...

White pyjamas
Black pyjamas
Cream pyjamas
Lime
Which colour pyjamas
Shall I wear for sleepy time?

Shall I choose...

Yellow pyjamas
Beige pyjamas
Orange pyjamas
Brown
Which colour pyjamas
Shall I wear to settle down?

Wait!
I know...

I don't have to choose a colour
I know what I'll wear instead
I've found my rainbow pyjamas
I'll wear a rainbow to bed!

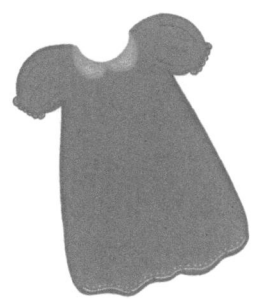

When I Am Crowned King

When I am crowned King
These things I will fix
Annoying things
Here is my list:

WATER!
The problem with water
Is that water is...wet
If water were jelly
In that bath I would get

PEAS!
The problem with peas
Is that peas are not...sweets
If peas were sweets
Every pea I would eat!

TOOTHPASTE!
The problem with toothpaste
Is that it's not...chocolate spread
If toothpaste were chocolate
I'd eat it on bread!

SCHOOL!
The problem with school
Is that it's not...much fun
If school were fun
To school I would RUN!

The world would be perfect
Except for these things
Can't wait to ban them
When I am crowned King!

Journey Of A Smile

I smiled today in the shop
To the lady next in the queue
Then something amazing happened
That smile just FLEW!

The lady smiled at the man next to her
Who smiled at the man selling meat
Who smiled at the lady buying fish
Who smiled at the child munching treats

Who smiled at the elderly man in a chair
Who smiled at the man wheeling him
Who smiled at the lady buying flowers
Who smiled at the child and her twin

Who smiled at the man selling meat
Who smiled at the man in the queue
Who smiled at the lady next to him
See how far my smile flew!

That one smile came back to me
That smile just multiplied
Give away a smile today
And watch it FLY! Fly! FLY!

Broccoli Price

Why is Broccoli Price named 'Broccoli'?
Well, it's very simple you see
Broccoli Price is completely obsessed
With the vegetable 'broccoli'

Broccoli Price
Broccoli Price
So in love with
Broccoli...nice!

He ate it for breakfast and lunch
He ate it for afternoon tea
He ate it for dinner and supper
So mad about broccoli!

Broccoli Price
Broccoli Price
So in love with
Broccoli...nice!

Broccoli Price looks quite ordinary
Though a tincy wincy bit green
He's eaten so much broccoli
He's the greenest man you will see!

Broccoli Price
Broccoli Price
So in love with
Broccoli...nice!

Broccoli Price wants a wife
Though he's searched the seven seas
There's no one he loves more in this world
Than his darling broccoli!

Broccoli Price
Broccoli Price
So in love with
Broccoli...nice!

Broccoli Price lives alone
In his cottage named Broccoli
But Broccoli Price could not be happier
With his darling broccoli

Broccoli Price
Broccoli Price
So in love with
Broccoli...NICE!

Eye Test

If you see a toad
With a heavy load
Crossing a road
You might need to have your eyes tested

If you see a frog
With a hedgehog
Going for a jog
You need to have your eyes tested

If you see a fish
Making a wish
In a casserole dish
You really need to have your eyes tested

If you see a goat
Writing Valentine notes
Afloat in a rowing boat
You really, really need to have your eyes tested

If you see a garden snail
With a killer whale
Drinking ginger ale
You really, really, really, need your eyes tested

If you see a giraffe
In a posh scarf
Having a bath
You really, really, really, really, need your eyes tested

If you see a deer
With a pierced ear
On a seaside pier
You really, really, really, really, really need your eyes tested!

(Have you made that appointment yet?)

Funny Poems

Write on your paper 'If you see a....' and see how many rhymes you can make. You can add the last line 'you need your eyes tested' at the end, too.

Help Me Write A Poem

Help me write a poem
About my birthday cake
The birthday cake my aunty made
And helped me decorate

Chocolate buttons, smarties
Juicy strawberry twists
Blueberries and caramel
Popping candy fizz

Jelly snakes and sour chews
Orange candy sticks
Lollipops and liquorice
Lemon sherbet dips

Help me write a poem
So I don't forget today
So the memory stays forever
And never fades away.

Listen

Listen to...
That sound from the kitchen
Squeak squeak squeak
Mouse is munching on cheese for supper
Squeak squeak squeak

Listen to...
That sound on the landing
Creak creak creak
Floor boards are yawning 'goodnight'
Creak creak creak

Listen to...
That sound at my window
Tap-tappity-tap
Branches are tapping 'sweet dreams'
Tap-tappity-tap

Listen to...
That sound through the key hole
Rat-a-tat-tat
Wind is rattling 'sleep tight, sleep tight'
Rat-a-tat-tat

Listen to...
That sound from my bed
Snore snore snore
Time to turn out the light
To snore, snore some more.

Great Fire Of London September 2nd 1666

We are live in London
With this breaking news
Flee from your homes
There's no time to lose

Flee! Flee!

A spark from an oven
Has caused a huge fire
It's sweeping the city
The situation is dire

Fire! Fire!

The flames were first seen
In Pudding Lane
People are saying
The baker's to blame

Roofs of straw
Houses of wood
Are fuelling this fire
The situation's not good

Crackle! Crackle!

Fill buckets of water
Every woman and man
Dampen those flames
As much as you can

Water! Water!

One week since the fire
The damage is done
We see tears in the eyes
Of everyone

St Paul's has fallen
Though it is made of stone
87 churches
Over 13,000 homes

Oh no! Oh no!

Strong winds fanned the fire
For four whole days
When the wind dropped
So did the flames

We hear from King Charles
That Christopher Wren
Will rebuild our city
Make it great again

And we must say thank you
To Mr Samuel Pepys
For recording history
In the diary he keeps

Thank you for watching
It is a tragic scene
The worst fire ever
That London has seen

We won't forget
The name Pudding Lane
Or the lesson it taught us
That fire is no game.

Goodnight. Keep safe.

Performance Tip
Have fun being a News Reporter but remember to use lots of 'facial expression' i.e. serious/shocked/sad.

Hello Children, Parents and Teachers

I hope you have enjoyed all the different poems in this book. As I said in my poem 'Just Write', there are so many different kinds of poems: funny, serious, sad, happy, thoughtful, silly, rhyming, non- rhyming and many more! Why not try writing your own poem?

Writing a Poem

Poems are just our thoughts on paper, so they really can be about anything at all. Look at some of the poems in this book which include writing tips on how to write your own poem. Don't forget to illustrate it.

Finding Rhymes

Poems don't have to rhyme, although one way to find rhymes is by listing the alphabet from A-Z down the side of your page. Say aloud the word you want to rhyme as you go down the list and write down all the rhyming words you can find next to each letter. You could even make your own notebook with a separate page for each letter. Soon you will have made your own book of rhymes which will be there whenever you need it!

Black's Rhyming and Spelling Dictionary by the poet Pie Corbett and non-fiction writer Ruth Thomson is also a great little book, used by lots of poets. Using it to find rhymes will also magically improve your spelling, reading and writing, too.

Learning a Poem

Read aloud one line at a time, and when you're sure of it, move on to the next line. Repeat each verse aloud before moving on to the next verse, so the words stick. Making up your own actions is also a fun way of remembering which line comes next.

Performing

There are lots of poems to perform in this book! If you're getting together with friends, decide who will perform which verse or line and what actions you will use. Don't forget we speak with our faces, too. Use loud and clear voices so everyone can hear you, and take your time.

Ready to go! Have fun!

Class Carpet Poems

Year 1s and Year 2s sit on the carpet for story time, circle time, and first thing in the morning for the register before going to their tables to work. These are poems that can be done on the carpet.

Thank You

Thank you to the poet Brian Moses who suggested many years ago I should write a book for younger children. I hope it's worth the wait, Brian. A massive thank you to Troika - it's been a pleasure working with you all. Thanks a million to the brilliantly talented illustrator Zoe Williams and designer Wendy Mach, who have brought not just the book but each poem to life with such wonderful illustrations and creative design.

Debra

PS I always love to hear from anyone who has enjoyed my poems. So, if you have learned or performed a poem of mine off by heart, or just loved reading my poems, I'd love to hear. Adults can contact me at www.debrabertulis.com or on Twitter at @DBertulis

About The Author

Debra Bertulis has been a writer of poetry, plays and stories since she was very young. When she was ten, her mother bought her a typewriter to type her stories on and she's been writing ever since. Her poems appear in many anthologies as well as on the LAMDA examination syllabus and are performed at Festivals across the world. Her debut collection of children's poetry, *Where Do Wishes Go*, was published in 2022.

See more about Debra at her website.

www.debrabertulis.com

About The Illustrator

Zoe is a master's student at the University of West England studying Graphic Arts. A doodler from day one, Zoe could always be found drawing, creating and thinking about new projects. *The Moon's Gorgonzola* (her favourite cheese) is her second collection of illustrations and showcases her love of animals and natural scenery. Her work is a combination of traditional drawing techniques and digital colouring. Defined by line, tone, and a sense of charm, her quirky characters invite readers into a world of imagination. Zoe plans to pursue a career as a freelance illustrator and hopes to contribute to more books in future!

See more about Zoe on her Instagram profile.

@zoe_portfolio_23

The home of great children's books

Troika is a small independent children's book publisher. We're based in the UK.

Follow us on social media

 @TroikaBooks

 @troikabooks

 @TroikaBooks